Beyond THE MIRROR

21 Days of Devotion, Affirmation, and Self-Love

MICHAL RENEE

KEEN
VISION
PUBLISHING

Limits of Liability and Disclaimer of Warranty

The author and publisher shall not be liable for your misuse of this material. This book is strictly for informational and educational purposes. The purpose of this book is to educate and entertain. The author and/or publisher do not guarantee that anyone following these techniques, suggestions, tips, ideas, or strategies will become successful. The author and/or publisher shall have neither liability nor responsibility to anyone with respect to any loss or damage caused, or alleged to be caused, directly or indirectly by the information contained in this book.

Views expressed in this publication do not necessarily reflect the views of the publisher.

Printed in the United States of America

ISBN: 978-0-9987200-1-2

Keen Vision Publishing, LLC

www.keen-vision.com

Dear Child,

I think the world of you.

Love,

God

acknowledgements

I have many influential people in my life. If I began to list everyone, this book would probably have an additional 50+ pages. First and foremost, I give all honor to God for loving me to wholeness. Our relationship has grown drastically over the last few years of my life. Though I can never pay You back for all You've done, my desire is to extend my gratitude to You through my service to Your people and unwavering commitment to Your will and purpose for my life. Understanding Your love for me has taught me how to love myself and others. God, I thank You!

To my parents, James and Annette Logan, thank you so much for how you raised me. Thank you for being Godly examples of a husband and wife. Thank you for being the best parents in the world despite everything life threw your way. Thank you for leading me to become the woman I am today. Daddy, thank you for paving the way and releasing your own book! Because you did it, I knew I could!

Thank you! To my mother, I thank you for always seeing the best in me, even when I couldn't see it myself. I love you guys!

To my siblings, thanks for being the best! I'm so grateful for your support. Thank you for the fun and laughter we've experienced through the years. I am so excited about what God is doing in each of your lives! Keep going! The best is yet to come!

To my friends and family, I love you guys dearly. Thank you for the phone calls, the Facebook shares/messages, and encouragement. You guys have been so instrumental in my life. I thank God for bringing each of you into my life when I needed it the most!

To Jessica D. Williams and the entire Keen Vision Publishing team, thank you so much for partnering with me on this endeavor to release my first book. I appreciate you guys!

Michal

about the author

"God has the last word. I'm just following His voice and doing what He tells me to do. This is my mission for as long as I have breath in my body."

-Michal Renee

Michal Renee Logan is a native of New Britain, Connecticut. She was raised in Huntsville, Alabama. Shortly after graduating high school, she moved to Plainville, Connecticut where she began her journey of finding God for herself and operating in her purpose. Michal was baptized for a second time on March 9, 2014. This second baptism meant a lot because she made the decision for herself after finally understanding what it meant to live a Godly life. It also represented the renewal of her relationship with God.

In 2015, she heard the voice of God prompting her to move back to Huntsville, AL. After moving back, she joined All Nations Christian Center under the leadership of Pastor Adrian Davis. That summer, she birthed Beauty For Ashes Ministries. It began as just a prayer call. Her goal is to establish Beauty for Ashes as a full ministry.

Michal is a licensed cosmetologist and makeup artist, but her passion is making women feel beautiful on the inside. Michal is currently pursuing a bachelor's degree in Pastoral Ministry at Huntsville Bible College. Beyond the Mirror is the first, but certainly not the last, book that will be written by Michal. She will continue to write as the Lord leads her.

contents

introduction

Before we begin, allow me to tell you a little about my life. I grew up with a big family. I'm the oldest of eight kids, my parents are still happily married, and I was born and raised in the church. Sounds like the perfect life, right? Outwardly, it looked like I had it all together. From the outside looking in, I had the perfect combination for a wholesome and healthy life. Everyone always assumed that I had it good. Most of my peers came from broken families and had no idea of how the inside of a church looked. When they looked at me, they didn't see any reason why I shouldn't be happy. Little did they know, I battled with so much growing up. I always felt like the oddball or the weird one.

From kindergarten to third grade, I dealt with bullying. Once I hit fourth grade, the bullying got worse and continued until I reached seventh grade. I have heard every ugly, dark-skinned, tall, and skinny joke imaginable. Kids can be pretty cruel, and the names they created for me were horrible. To make matters worse, my name is Michal, pronounced Michael. All the kids got a kick out of me being a girl with a masculine name. Boys would hit me and make fun of me. The girls would giggle at their every joke and refuse to be my friend. I felt like the girls who pretended to be my friends betrayed me when they would laugh along with whatever new joke the guys created. For quite some time, I faced difficulty trusting female friends.

I lived in a strict household, and fighting wasn't acceptable. I didn't want to disappoint my parents, so I didn't react to the bullying. I just dealt with it. Kids called me ugly and dark-skinned so much that I created this monster image of myself in my mind and refused to go near a mirror. I was terrified that I would see what everyone else was calling me. I had very low self-esteem.

By the time I went to high school, I was pretty much chewed up and spit out. My grades weren't that great, I was mean, and had a ten-foot wall around me. In fear that I would be teased, I kept to myself and rarely talked to my classmates and peers. I often worried about who I could trust.

There were guys I had a crush on, but I never even looked their way because I knew I didn't have a chance with them. Around this time, I began to have issues at home. The side effects of the bullying carried over into every area of my life. More than anything, I wanted to get away from Huntsville and start my life over.

Eventually, I moved back to my birthplace, Connecticut. I came out of my shell, and I loved it! After six years of living in Connecticut, God said it was time for me to go back home. I didn't want to, but I knew it was time. I was spiritually mature enough to know that I couldn't disobey God. Though I was very reluctant, I made my journey back to Huntsville, AL.

In June 2016, I had the opportunity to take vocal lessons with Jamel Strong. At every session, we had to stand in front of a mirror, look at ourselves breathe, and make sure we were opening our mouths wide enough. One day, Jamel mentioned to me that I was not looking in the mirror. I didn't realize that I had been avoiding looking at myself. He and I went through an entire class going back and forth about looking in the mirror. I went home to practice singing in the mirror, and that lasted all of thirty seconds. I cried like a baby and asked God what was wrong with me. I couldn't understand why I was having a hard time looking at myself in the mirror. As I prayed for answers, God reminded me of my past. He showed me how I never dealt with it.

As a licensed hair stylist and professional makeup artist, I was constantly looking in the mirror. I didn't understand what the big deal was. The Holy Spirit revealed to me that every time I looked in the mirror, I viewed myself as someone else, my alter ego. Since I didn't deal with everything that took place when I was a child, the hurt and pain carried over into my adulthood. By running to Connecticut, I subconsciously placed band aids on wounds that needed stitches.

One day, I woke up and decided that enough was enough. I was sick of my past holding me hostage. I was tired of being unable to move forward in all God had in store for me. After God walked me through the process of loving myself again, I soon realized that I wasn't the only one who dealt with self-esteem issues. The Holy Spirit led me to write this book, Beyond the Mirror.

I've told you my story, and now I want you to take a second and think about your story. How do you view yourself? Don't think about the person you pretend to be in front of others. Take away the looks, hair, contacts, and glasses. Think about who you are when you are home alone. What are the thoughts you think of yourself?

If we were honest, we all would admit that we deal with low self-esteem in some area of our lives. Maybe you don't like your nose. Maybe you hate the way your eyes look. For some of you, it may be deeper. Maybe you don't like the way you process your thoughts. Or, maybe you don't like the way sound when you talk. Regardless of how you deal with low self-esteem, my desire is to walk you through the process of seeing yourself the way God sees you.

This book is a 21-day devotional filled with self-compliments and affirmations. Before we can ever be all God has created us to be, we must be confident about the person we see in the mirror and the person beyond the mirror. No matter how many times people tell us how amazing we are, we won't see it until we are confident in who God has created us to be.

Throughout the next 21 days, I challenge you to be real, raw, and authentic with yourself. Allow your heart to be open to every confirmation and affirmation you read. Take each one and recite it to yourself throughout the designated day. It may feel weird at first, but keep going.

As you build yourself in God's truth about you, you will be able to accept and appreciate who you are. Each day has a BTM (Beyond the Mirror) Challenge and a prayer starter. Use the prayer starters to begin your conversation with God about each affirmation. Use the challenges to take action towards believing the truth about you! This journey will be amazing. At the end of these 21 days, my prayer is that you will be able to look in and beyond the mirror with confidence. If you are ready, turn the page and let's begin!

day one

I am Loved by God

"For I am convinced that neither death nor life, neither angels nor demons, neither the present nor the future, nor any powers, neither height nor depth, nor anything else in all creation, will be able to separate us from the love of God that is in Christ Jesus our Lord."

Romans 8:38-39 (NIV)

I am loved by God. Sounds pretty cliché, huh? We hear this saying pretty often, but do we really receive all that it encompasses? Being loved by God is such a big deal when we think of how unlovable we can be at times. We do things outside of His Will and still expect His provision. We tell Him we will change and never do. We put Him on hold and don't pick up the phone until we need Him to handle the next big thing. We repent and go back to the same lifestyle. Even in all of this, He still loves us. Again, God's love is a big deal. There is nothing cliché about it. Sadly, we have grown accustomed to looking for love in all the wrong places instead of allowing God's love to fulfill us. We are hurt by the superficial love we sought after because we never first understood the love of God. When we truly know and accept God's love for us, it's difficult to fall for superficial love from other places. So, before we take another step, let us affirm ourselves in God's love for us. Before we learn how to love ourselves, we must realize who loved us first. God's love is the standard by which all love should be measured.

PRAYER STARTER God, thank You for Your unfailing love. Thank You for loving me so much that You give me chance after chance to get it right. Thank You for showing me my worth. I know that when everyone turns their backs on me, You will still love and support me by giving me all that I need. The truth is, I'll never know how much You really love me, but I ask that You help me to see Your love daily.

BTM CHALLENGE Instead of your usual shopping trip with the girls, or playing ball with the fellas, schedule sometime this week to go on a date with God. You can go to dinner and a movie, or just sit at home. Be intentional about enjoying God's presence. Be sure to write down everything God shares with you during this time.

Journaling Beyond the Mirror

day two

God Has Forgiven Me

"Therefore, if anyone is in Christ, the new creation has come: The old has gone, the new is here! All this is from God, who reconciled us to himself through Christ and gave us the ministry of reconciliation;"

2 Corinthians 5:17-18 (NIV)

Do you know one perfect person? Can you say you know one person who does absolutely everything right? Me either. Since we know perfection in this life doesn't exist, why do we have a hard time forgiving ourselves when we make mistakes? Furthermore, why do we have a hard time accepting God's forgiveness? If God, our Creator and Father, can forgive us, why can't we forgive ourselves? God doesn't forgive us for us to continue to beat ourselves up! Guilt and condemnation are not of God. He doesn't want us to feel guilty about our mistakes. Instead, He desires us to be convicted to change. Guilt and condemnation are among the major reasons many people have low self-esteem. Today, make the decision to receive God's forgiveness and forgive yourself. You can't go back and change the things you've done, but you can move forward and do better with God's grace!

PRAYER STARTER Lord, forgive me for not forgiving myself. I silence the sound of condemnation and guilt in my mind. Help me learn how to forgive myself immediately and not allow unforgiveness to linger. Forgiveness is a gift You have given me, and I thank You for it.

BTM CHALLENGE Write a letter to yourself. Ask God to reveal everything you have been holding against yourself. As you write, forgive yourself for everything. Write about how you will move forward into your future.

Journaling Beyond the Mirror

My Past Is Wrong About Me

"Therefore, if anyone is in Christ, the new creation has come: The old has gone, the new is here!"

2 Corinthians 5:17 (NIV)

Everyone has a past. Our pasts make us unique. Whether good or bad, our pasts taught us lessons that will prove to be very beneficial in our futures. Though our pasts may have contributed to the person we are today, they do not define us. They do not give us a name. The moment we accepted Christ into our lives, we were given new lives in Him. Does this mean that we should forget our story? Absolutely not. Scripture tells us that we are overcomers by the blood of the lamb and the words of our testimonies (Revelation 12:11). Our testimonies have the power to help unbelievers believe, teach the unfaithful how to have faith, and encourage those who have reached the end of their rope to endure. As we enjoy our newness in Christ, we must share our testimonies with others so that they too can find their newness in Christ! How can we help others with our testimonies if we still feel bound to our past mistakes? We can't. Today, declare that your past does not define you! When the enemy taunts you about the things you once did, the places you once visited, and the people you once entertained, laugh and let hell know that you don't do those things anymore! Instead of allowing hell's reminder of your past to make you feel bad, allow it to motivate you to help other people.

PRAYER STARTER God, thank You for being a restorer. Because of You, my past can not haunt me! Thank You for giving me a new name. Lord, help me not to be ashamed of my past. I was not perfect, and I'm still not perfect, but I serve a perfect God. Give me the courage to tell my story to others so that they may grow closer to you.

BTM CHALLENGE Write your testimony. Take a moment and reflect on where God has brought you from. Challenge yourself to find at least one person with whom you can share your testimony.

Ask God to lead you to the person who could benefit from hearing your story.

Journaling Beyond the Mirror

day four

I Am Not Afraid

"For God has not given us a spirit of fear, but of power and of love and of a sound mind."

2 Timothy 1:7 (NKJV)

Since I was a little girl, I've always been afraid of something – the dark, bugs, animals, people, singing publicly, you name it. When I questioned God about my fear, He gave me a vision of myself wrapped in chains. The chains represented fear. Fear is dangerous. In the natural, when we are afraid, we become very still. Fear causes us to stop in our tracks. It impacts us the same in the spirit. Spiritually, fear causes us not to move forward and to become stagnant. Everyone doesn't battle inconsistency or discipline. Some of us simply deal with fear. We know what to do, and we know how to do it, but fear of our own success freezes us every time. Our scripture for today shows us that fear is not from God. All we need to defeat fear, is power, love, and a sound mind.

Whenever we start to feel fear rise, we only need to think of this bible verse, use what God has given us, and cast out fear in the name of Jesus.

PRAYER STARTER I bind and rebuke the spirit of fear, in Jesus' name! Fear will no longer hold me bound. Fear will no longer be an option! I will walk in love, power, and a sound mind. God, thank You for being with me. I have no reason to be afraid.

BTM CHALLENGE Write down the things you are afraid to do. List your extreme fears (bungee jumping, skydiving, jumping out of a plane, roller coasters, etc.) Then, list your smaller fears (trying different foods, getting a new haircut, going to the doctor, etc.) Schedule sometime this week (or in the near future) to conquer one of your small fears. After you conquer a small fear, challenge yourself to knock out one of the bigger ones! Be sure to journal your experience and share it on social media using the hashtag, #BTMCHALLENGE. Who knows? You just might encourage others to leap over their fears too!

Journaling Beyond the Mirror

day five

I Have the Strength to Move on

"but those who hope in the Lord will renew their strength. They will soar on wings like eagles; they will run and not grow weary they will walk and not be faint."

Isaiah 40:31 (NIV)

Healing is a process. Sometimes we are hurt so badly and so deeply that we want the pain to go away quickly. When it doesn't go away, we find ourselves covering it with a new "whatever hurt us last time." I'll give you a few examples:

- A new relationship after a relationship goes bad.
- A new best friend when we are at odds with our friends.
- A new habit after we get rid of other habits.

When we are hurt, we do whatever we can to help us forget the pain. Of course, this never works. Nine times out of ten, we find ourselves with more pain than when we began. Here's the thing:

Healing is a day by day process. It takes intentional time in the presence of God. It isn't always easy. There are days in which we will move through easily, and there are days we will want to give up. On those rough days, we don't have to pull from our own strength! Honestly, we don't have the strength to get through difficult things on our own. There's only so much we can give until we are burnt out! We must condition our minds to place our hope in God. We must depend on Him to give us the strength we need to endure the journey of healing. This is the only way we can effectively make it through the healing process.

PRAYER STARTER God, thank You for helping me to endure and giving me the strength to do so. Honestly, some days I don't even want to get out of the bed. On those days, I trust You to give me the strength to keep going. When times get hard, remind me to trust You. Remind me that in You, I can do all things.

BTM CHALLENGE Sometimes, we don't have spiritual strength because we don't have physical strength. Today go for a walk or even a jog. While you're walking or jogging, meditate and listen to what God has to say about your situation.

Journaling Beyond the Mirror

day six

My Ways Are Not God's Ways

"For my thoughts are not your thoughts, neither are your ways my ways," declares the Lord. "As the heavens are higher than the earth, so are my ways higher than your ways and my thoughts than your thoughts."

Isaiah 55:8-9 (NIV)

We've all heard the saying, "The best way to make God laugh is to tell Him your plans." Much of our low self-esteem comes from plans that did not go the way we desired them to go. Instead of feeling like a failure, challenge yourself to think about everything you view as a failure. Was it God's will in the first place? Did it align with God's will for your life? As we walk into our calling, we must remember that though it may be OUR calling, it was God who called us in the first place. We didn't call ourselves. In fact, many of us ran when we realized God called us! When we allow ourselves to get so high on the horse and never consider God's plans for our lives, things won't go well – no matter how great of an idea they may be. We must surrender our will to God daily. He has so much in store for us, but we limit what we receive when we don't trust God's plan. We think about the right now, but God designed a plan for our lives that will far surpass the years and generations to come. I don't know about you, but I'm glad I wasn't given the responsibility of planning my entire life. I would have left out some people, places, and things that were vital to my future. Release the stress of trying to figure it all out, and trust God who has already figured it out.

PRAYER STARTER God, I thank You so much that Your ways and Your thoughts are nothing like my own. Help me adjust my thoughts and ways to fit Yours. Guide me in my decisions. Remind me that You are always in control no matter what the situation looks like.

BTM CHALLENGE I know you've probably planned tomorrow out with to-do lists, meetings, and work, but I challenge you to ask God what He would like you to do tomorrow. Once you give it a try, make it a habit of including God in your plans. Don't write anything in your planner, or put anything in your Google calendar until God has approved it.

Journaling Beyond the Mirror

day seven

I Will Take Rest in God

"In vain you rise early and stay up late, toiling for food to eat—for he grants sleep to those he loves."

Psalm 127:2 (NIV)

Today is for the workaholics – those of you who work, work, work, and never take the time to relax and enjoy life. Believe it or not, this may be a result of having low self-esteem. Most workaholics feel as though they have something to prove, so they work relentlessly to prove it. Don't get me wrong, there's nothing wrong with being a hard worker, but we must be sure to check our motives for working so hard. Who are you competing with? What are you trying to prove? We all need rest. When we rest, God restores us, speaks to us, and gives us strategy for the next season of our lives. It's great to be disciplined, but we must also learn to take rest when we need it. Believe it or not, there are some people who feel bad when they take breaks. If you are one of those people, understand this is only a trick of the enemy. The enemy desires us to be so tired that we cannot fight when he sends trouble our way. This cannot be so! As you work hard to carry out the tasks and assignments of God, you must also remember to rest! After you are fully rested, go back to your work knowing that you are restored and prepared to keep pressing towards the mark!

PRAYER STARTER God, I'm afraid of being broke. I'm afraid of not being good enough. As a result, I've pushed myself hard, and I have not taken the time to rest in you. Help me to understand that you provide my needs. No matter how hard I work, I can make nothing happen for myself. It is You who provides my needs. Remind me to take breaks when I need them. Protect my thoughts when I sleep and help me to rest throughout the night.

BTM CHALLENGE Make some time to do an activity you know calms you. For example, you could go swimming, take a walk, schedule a massage or facial, go to the gym, cook, get your hair done, or get a pedicure/manicure. During this time, turn your phone off, force yourself to not think about work, and relax! As you relax, listen to God. Journal what you hear and get back to work!

Journaling Beyond the Mirror

day eight

I Don't Need Their Approval

"Am I now trying to win the approval of human beings, or of God? Or am I trying to please people? If I were still trying to please people, I would not be a servant of Christ."

Galatians 1:10 (NIV)

Growing up, I was NEVER accepted. I was always in search of the friendship, love, and company of others to confirm who I was. I was always looking for the approval of others. I wanted the approval of my teachers, my family, and my peers. As a result, I did things I wasn't comfortable with and changed myself to fit their desires. I changed so much and so often that I didn't even know who I was. One day, I realized that everyone I met would have their standards and preferences, but I could not change to meet each one. I had to stay true to who God created me to be. I had to stay true to Michal. I encourage you to do the same. Stop trying to please people who are always changing. Our desire should be to please God. He is always the same. His love is always the same. His Word is always the same. He never changes. When we work to please people, we find ourselves empty, but when we work to please God, He strengthens, confirms, and restores us as we work!

PRAYER STARTER God, I thank You that I do not need the approval of other people! All of my life, I have searched for the approval of man. Now, I will use that same energy to please You! You have already approved me. I will rest and find peace in knowing that You are all I need. Thank You for confirming me. Thank You for loving me. Thank you for restoring me. Thank You for saving me from the approval of others.

BTM CHALLENGE What have you been avoiding because of a lack of support from others? Today, I challenge you to pull those plans out of the closet, blow the dust off of them, and get to work. Here's the only rule. You can't tell anyone about it until it is complete. During this time, allow God to be your guide, your accountability partner, and your support. Be sure to journal your experience! Take note of the difference between working for God's approval vs. the approval of others.

Journaling Beyond the Mirror

day nine

I Love Me Some Me!

"Love is patient, love is kind. It does not envy, it does not boast, it is not proud. It does not dishonor others, it is not self-seeking, it is not easily angered, it keeps no record of wrongs. Love does not delight in evil but rejoices with the truth. It always protects, always trusts, always hopes, always perseveres."

1 Corinthians 13:4-7 (NIV)

This bible verse isn't just about how to love others. It also provides insight on how we should love ourselves. Sometimes, we treat others better than we treat ourselves. We find it easy to be patient with others, but we feel as though we must get it together overnight. We are quick to compliment someone else, but when we look in the mirror, we can't seem to find anything nice to say. One way to beat low self-esteem is to treat ourselves the way God treats us. We must love ourselves with the same care and intentionality as God loves us. We are His creation. We can't fully operate in His love or love others when we don't love ourselves. Loving ourselves isn't about being selfish. Loving ourselves is about appreciating what God has done and how He has created us. Loving ourselves is refusing to speak negatively about who we are, how we perform, how we look, and how we progress. When we speak negatively of ourselves, we are speaking negatively of God. Remember, He is Our Creator.

PRAYER STARTER Thank You, God, for teaching me how to love me! Loving You is showing me how to love myself. Continue to show me how to love the creation You have made perfect! My skin color, my eyes, my body, my hair, my smile, my personality, and MY STORY are good because everything You make is good. Help me to be patient and kind to myself.

BTM CHALLENGE Stop what you are doing and take a selfie. No, don't fix your hair. Don't put on lip gloss. Take the picture just as you are and post it on social media using the hashtag, #iLovemesomeme. Don't do it for likes, to start a trend, or for the approval of others. Do it because you truly love you, just as you are, wherever you are, and however you are!

Journaling Beyond the Mirror

day ten

I Am Fulfilled!

"You make known to me the path of life; you will fill me with joy in your presence, with eternal pleasures at your right hand."

Psalm 16:11 (NIV)

I don't know about you, but I have tried all types of things to satisfy myself and fill the voids in my life. Relationships, of course, being the main thing. I found temporary love, which turned out not to be love at all. I would leave one situation after another in my search for fulfillment and satisfaction. One day, I got tired and cried out for God's help. I learned that when we experience God's love and the fullness thereof, we don't have to search for anything else because He loves us so much! In order to feel completely satisfied and fulfilled, we must allow God to fill the empty places in our hearts. When we refuse to allow God's love to fill the void, we have unrealistic expectations of others. It doesn't matter how great a person is, they are still not God. No one can love you the way He does. Until you allow God to fill the voids in your life, no one else will ever satisfy you.

PRAYER STARTER Dear God, I have tried everything to fill the empty spaces in my heart. Now, I know You are all the fulfillment I need. Thank You for filling up those empty spaces in my heart. Thank You for loving me and working with me. I am so grateful for Your love that makes me complete!

BTM CHALLENGE Did you know that serving others can help fill the voids we feel in our hearts? Contact your local soup kitchen or shelter and volunteer. You will enjoy the humbling experience. Additionally, the love and compassion you feel from serving others will fill your heart with joy.

Journaling Beyond the Mirror

day eleven

I Am Already Better

"See, I am doing a new thing! Now it springs up; do you not perceive it? I am making a way in the wilderness and streams in the wasteland."

Isaiah 43:19 (NIV)

Let's be honest. Sometimes, we just don't give ourselves enough credit! After we've experienced years and years of failure, it can be hard to see our growth and maturity. This not only affects how we see ourselves, but it also affects how we see God. Our God isn't a statue that sits still. Our God is always working and moving. We can't see how He is moving if we only focus on what the negative parts of our lives. Sure, we haven't done everything right, but look at what we did do right. Think about this. Are you the same person you were last week, last month, or last year? Of course not! Something about you has changed for the good. Today, I challenge you to look at how you've changed. Don't look externally.

Look beyond what you can see in the mirror. Take some time and meditate on all the work God has done in your life. Challenge yourself to highlight the positives. You will find that you are much further than you thought you were.

PRAYER STARTER Lord, I'll be the first to admit that I'm far from perfect. Lately, my mistakes have made me feel like less of a person. Help me to see how I have changed. Help me to see the areas in which I have improved. God, give me the strength to endure the new thing you are doing in my life even now.

BTM CHALLENGE Are you ready for more social media fun? Let's go!

Step One: Find a picture of who you once were.

Step Two: Take a picture of the new and improved you!

Step Three: Combine the pictures in a collage and post it on your favorite social media site using the hashtag, #old2newBTM. Be sure to share your testimony!

Journaling Beyond the Mirror

day twelve

I'm Different and That's Okay

"Do not conform to the pattern of this world, but be transformed by the renewing of your mind. Then you will be able to test and approve what God's will is—his good, pleasing and perfect will."

Romans 12:2 (NIV)

I always thought something was wrong with me. I was always the black sheep, and I never fit in. Being a part of a clique? You can forget it! I always felt like God purposely caused me to stand out to remind me that I was different from everyone else. When we think about being different, we often think about our outer appearance. Let's look beyond the mirror. We have unique mindsets, goals, views, opinions, desires, and needs. And guess what? That's okay! Here's the thing. If God wanted us all to look alike, dress alike, sound alike, think alike, and talk alike, He could have done just that, but He didn't! He made us different – even down to the prints on our fingers. Each of us must be who God created us to be. Once we accept our uniqueness, we can begin walking in our destinies with confidence. God has a perfect plan for you, but He needs YOU to do it. So many of us have blended our lives with the opinions and delights of others that we barely even know who we are anymore. There is a blessing in being who God created you to be! Every day, we must strive to be the person He fashioned in the heavens, not a carbon copy of what we see on Earth.

PRAYER STARTER God, thank You for making me different. You have given me the grace to be me. I'm so grateful that I don't have to fit in. Thank You for giving me the confidence to be me. Teach me to be appreciative of the unique gift You have given me. Thank You for creating me to be a trendsetter.

BTM CHALLENGE We all have that one thing that sets us apart from everyone else. Today, spend some time journaling about what makes you, YOU! After you are done, find a frame and slide in your journal entry. Keep it somewhere visible.

Remind yourself often that you are different and that's okay!

Journaling Beyond the Mirror

day thirteen

I Forgive

"And when you stand praying, if you hold anything against anyone, forgive them, so that your Father in heaven may forgive you your sins."

Mark 11:25 (NIV)

Forgiveness is always a tough conversation. It's not easy to forgive someone who has hurt us, however, forgiveness is necessary if we ever hope to move past the pain. True healing begins with forgiveness. Unforgiveness affects our spiritual walk and our relationship with God. Did you know that there are case studies that link grudges and unforgiveness to stomach illnesses, heart failures, and cancer? Many of us have fooled ourselves into thinking that it is easier to hold a grudge than to forgive. I challenge you to think about that! Think about the work that goes into ignoring someone, being short with someone, avoiding someone, etc. It's hard work to be mean and hateful to those who have hurt us. I don't know about you, but I don't have time to be intentionally unforgiving. We have to forgive in order to move on and be at peace. Holding on to pain not only affects us, but it affects the generations that come after us. Who wants to plant seeds of bitterness in their future generation? So how do we forgive? It's simple. We let go. Forgiveness does not mean reconciliation. Just because you forgive someone does not mean you should welcome them back into your life. It simply means that you release what they have done to you. Challenge yourself to walk through the process of forgiving today. You'll be so glad you did!

PRAYER STARTER God, you have forgiven me. I have forgiven myself. Now, I forgive every person who has wronged me. I don't want to walk in unforgiveness anymore. I want to be free. Teach me how to forgive instantly. I don't want to keep bitterness in my heart. If you can forgive me, then I can forgive others too.

BTM CHALLENGE Who are you holding a grudge against? It's time to let it go. Don't wait until tomorrow. Do it now! First, ask God to walk you through the process of forgiving them in your heart. Next, take action. Write a letter, send a text, or make a phone call! Do whatever you can to clear the air. If the person you need to forgive is deceased, write a letter. After you've taken action, ask God to forgive you for harboring unforgiveness in your heart. Forgiveness is a process. So whenever you feel those angry feelings creeping back in, remind yourself that you have already forgiven them! Let the healing process begin!

Journaling Beyond the Mirror

day fourteen

It is Well

"Please run now to meet her and say to her, 'Is it well with you? Is it well with your husband? Is it well with the child?'" And she answered, "It is well."

2 Kings 4:26(NASB)

A while ago, my Pastor's spiritual father preached a message titled, "It is well!" He taught from a story in 2 Kings 4 about a woman who was married and couldn't have children. One day, a prophet of God told her she was going to have a son. She had the son, and he died a few years later. She was distraught. She decided to see the prophet. On her way there, she ran into the prophet's assistant who asked her if everything was okay. Her response was, "It is well."

Oftentimes when we go through difficult seasons, we speak negatively about the rest of our lives. We find ourselves saying, "I just can't catch a break!" Or, "Something is always going wrong!" There is power in our language. When situations are bad, we have two options. We can speak life into them, or we can speak death into them. We must be cautious about our response in difficult times. What sense would it make to curse the rest of our lives because of how we feel in one little moment of our lives?

At the end of the story, the woman's son came back to life. This story might have been a little different if her response had not been, "It is well." Now, I challenge you to think about your own lives. How could your response to a situation change the entire situation? Now that we understand that God is doing a new thing in our lives, we can no longer speak death into our situations. God allows us to go through tests not only to get the glory, but to also teach us how to respond.

PRAYER STARTER Gracious God, show me how to speak well over unpleasant situations that I don't understand. I know that the power of life and death is in my tongue. Show me how to speak life over my situations. Teach me how to be more intentional about the words that come out of my mouth. I may not see anything happening at that moment, but I will stand on Your word and believe that everything will work together for my good!

BTM CHALLENGE Today, watch your words! It may sound simple, but it's not as easy as you think. Listen to what comes out of your mouth. To make things a little bit more interesting, get a piggy bank or a mason jar and label it, "It Is Well." Each time you speak negatively, drop in a quarter. At the end of the day, count up the cost of your negativity. Do this every day until you make a habit of being cautious about what comes out of your mouth.

Journaling Beyond the Mirror

day fifteen

God's Peace Surrounds My Life

"And the peace of God, which transcends all understanding, will guard your hearts and your minds in Christ Jesus."

Philippians 4:7 (NIV)

When we overthink and overstress, one thing is evident: We do not trust God. Peace means freedom from internal and external strife. If we continue to overthink, we will never have peace. Having the peace of God that surpasses all understanding means that absolutely nothing has to make sense. When we allow ourselves to stop forcing everything to make sense, we will find peace. God wants us to be at peace so we can hear Him. If we're not at peace, it's hard to hear God over the noise of our concerns. Sometimes, our peace is held up because of others, but more often than not, we are our own peace thieves. Today, lay aside every burden, pray, and release your worries over to God. Only He can provide you with the peace you need to hear clear instructions for this season of your life!

PRAYER STARTER Thank You, God, for allowing me to experience Your peace. Thank You for granting me the opportunity to feel Your peace when I put my trust in You. I'm thankful that in a world full of craziness, Your peace surrounds my life!

BTM CHALLENGE What's been causing you not to have peace? Pinpoint what is stressing you out, and pray about it. After you pray, intentionally release the stress and worry to God. Over the next few days, continue to pray. Journal how God begins to work everything out for you!

Journaling Beyond the Mirror

day sixteen

I Choose Peace!

"Do not be anxious about anything, but in every situation, by prayer and petition, with thanksgiving, present your requests to God."

Philippians 4:6 (NIV)

Everything we do is a choice. We can choose to be anxious, or we can choose to be at peace. Many of us choose anxiety, stress, and worry because it's what we are accustomed to. Worrying about a situation doesn't show God how concerned you are, it shows God how much you don't trust who He is.

Our controlling minds feel as though it's better to worry than to be at peace. Everything that concerns us concerns God, but in this scripture, He shows us how to give our concerns to Him. We must do so through prayer.

Notice, the scripture tells us not to worry before it tells us to pray. This is very important. We must be careful not to go into prayer with doubtful hearts.

God gave us free will in every area of our lives. He won't force us to be at peace, but once we choose to be at peace, He allows us to enter His rest. We must meet Him halfway. He can't make that decision for us. Today, make the decision to be at peace!

PRAYER STARTER Lord, thank You for the choice of being at peace! I refuse to sit around and worry. Enough is enough! I choose to be at peace this day and every day of my life. I will not be anxious. I will not be afraid. I will not be worried. I will not stress out. I choose to be at peace!

BTM CHALLENGE Think of the very thing that drives you crazy and worries you. Write it down. Then, decree and declare peace over that situation and give it to God. Remember, you can't take it back once you give it to God and choose to be at peace. Be sure to journal how God works the situation out for you.

Journaling Beyond the Mirror

day seventeen

I Won't Give Up

"My flesh and my heart may fail, but God is the strength of my heart and my portion forever."

Psalm 73:26 (NIV)

We've all experienced failure in our lives. Some of us have experienced so much failure that we are afraid to try again. I'm going to let you in on a little secret: You haven't failed until you give up! Choosing to give up steals our chance to ever succeed. We must decide today that we will not give up. I don't care how many times you've tried to get it right, don't give up until you do! Don't you know that the greatest successes are usually accompanied by the greatest tests? If you give up now, you will never know all that you could have accomplished. As the saying goes, if at first you don't succeed, try again! Keep trying until you get it right. Understand that the failure you experience along the way is only a lesson on how you can do better next time! Think about all the amazing inventions that we use today. Do you think they were created by just one shot? Just look at Apple products. The first phones had issues, but that pushed Apple to go back to the drawing board and improve! They release new phones often, and each is better than the one before. Now, think about you. What remedies, ideas, inventions, or businesses are you holding? Have you been sitting on something that could possibly change the world? You will never know if you give up. Today, push yourself to give your idea another shot. Then, another shot. Then, another shot. Whatever you do, don't give up.

PRAYER STARTER I declare that I am not a failure! I bind up every generational curse of giving up, and I loose persistence over my life even now in the name of Jesus. Thank You for giving me the grace to keep going. Help me to keep going even when I want to give up. I come against every negative word spoken over my life. Help me to speak life into my situations. I will not fail because You have never failed me.

BTM CHALLENGE Think of something you did not finish because you thought you were going to fail. Write it down and ask God to help you start over again. Pray for strategy and develop an action plan. Make up your mind that no matter what happens this time around, you will not give up!

Journaling Beyond the Mirror

day eighteen

I Am an Overcomer

"Blessed is the one who perseveres under trial because, having stood the test, that person will receive the crown of life that the Lord has promised to those who love him."

James 1:12 (NIV)

God never promised that life would be easy. Even Jesus Christ experienced turmoil and obstacles, so why on earth do we believe that we should be excluded from tribulation? Here's the beautiful thing about the obstacles we face: Even though the enemy designed them to kill us, God allows them so we can prepare for what is ahead! Every obstacle we face is simply training ground for where God wants to take us. It is through conquering obstacles that we gain the strength to retain what God gives us. Just think about it this way. Many are better stewards because they know what it's like to not have anything. Some are more grateful for their spouses because of the heartbreak they experienced in the past. Some know how to remain humble in success because they know what it feels like to fail. Today, I encourage you to keep pressing towards the mark. You are an overcomer. You will get through this obstacle just like you got over the last obstacle. Take a moment and think about how you got through everything you thought was going to take you out. Look at you now! You are still here! The enemy's tricks didn't work last time, and they won't work this time. Look in the mirror and tell yourself, "I am an overcomer!"

PRAYER STARTER With you by my side, I have overcome every obstacle in my life. I will continue to overcome! I am stronger, and I am better. I thank You for every test and trial that have come my way because they brought me closer to You. I declare that hell is under my feet. I will continue to fight the good fight! I will continue to overcome!

BTM CHALLENGE Think of every obstacle the Lord has brought you through. Write them down. Next, think of someone you know who is currently trying to overcome an obstacle. Pray for them, and ask God to give them the strength to overcome. Send them an encouraging text or email to let them know that they will get through!

Journaling Beyond the Mirror

day nineteen

I'm No Longer Bound

"S,o if the Son sets you free, you will be free indeed."

John 8:36 (NIV)

When Jesus Christ died on the cross, He paid the price for our freedom. Understand that you owe nothing to be free. It doesn't matter what you struggle with, where you fall short, or how you mess up. You can be free. Bondage defines anything that enslaves us. We can be bound by unforgiveness, hatred, ignorance, bitterness, laziness, inconsistency, etc. The list goes on. Here's the beautiful part of our story: It doesn't matter what we are bound by, Jesus Christ paid the price for it all! All we must do is confess with our mouths and believe in our hearts that Jesus Christ died on the cross for our sins. Just like that, we are free! God desires each of us to get free and stay free. He desired this so much that He sent His only begotten Son to pay the price for our freedom. Will you receive His freedom today?

PRAYER STARTER God, I know I haven't always walked in freedom, but today, I'm turning over a new leaf. I believe in my heart that Jesus Christ died on the cross for my sins. I believe that His sacrifice set me free from everything that has held me bound. I receive my freedom today. Give me the strength to live a life that is pleasing to you. Guide me to people who can help me along the way.

BTM CHALLENGE Hey you! Dance! Find your favorite song and let loose. Even if you don't have rhythm, shake your hands and move your feet until you feel the breaking of every chain that has bound you. Dance until you realize that you are free!

Journaling Beyond the Mirror

day twenty

I Will Receive Beauty for Ashes!

"To all who mourn in Israel, he will give a crown of beauty for ashes, a joyous blessing instead of mourning, festive praise instead of despair. In their righteousness, they will be like great oaks that the Lord has planted for his own glory."

Isaiah 61:3 (NIV)

Back in the day, it was Jewish custom to pour ashes over your body when you were mourning or repenting. Ashes represented desolation and ruin. Though we don't physically pour ashes over ourselves, many of us still hold on to this ancient practice by filling our minds with thoughts of desolation and ruin.

After experiencing so much turmoil, we often wallow in our grief and disappointment. We begin to ask God, "Why me? Where are You? I thought You said You would never leave or forsake me." Even though we question Him in our tough seasons, God still gives us beauty for our ashes. Isn't He such a loving God? Despite how we felt, when it's all over, we get to trade in our sorrows and pain for the joy of the Lord.

The next time you are faced with a difficult situation, remind yourself that in the good, bad, ugly, and indifferent, God is right there. Know that everything will work together for your good. He will get the Glory for everything we have endured! Knowing that there is beauty for our ashes should encourage us to share our testimonies with others, instead of covering them up! It's great to talk about the joy, overflow, and abundance, but don't leave out the sorrow, lack, and deficiencies you traded in to get them! That's the best part of the story!

PRAYER STARTER God, I know this may sound crazy, but thank You for making me the example. Thank You for using me to show people Your love, grace, and mercy. Thank You for using me to show others how You give us beauty for ashes. I know that everything I've endured was for a reason. I know that my testimony is going to help others in a tremendous way. Give me the strength to tell my story. Lead me to the ones who need to hear it.

BTM CHALLENGE Do you remember when we were younger (in the days of rotary phones for some of us) whenever we wanted to get the juicy details for gossip or find out if someone really liked us, we would get our friend to call and ask them on three-way? Well today, we are going to put those three-way calling skills to good use. Pick three people you know and three-way call each other. On the call, allow each person to share their testimony. You are included! After everyone is done, allow everyone to share how the testimonies have encouraged them to keep going. Journal your experience!

Journaling Beyond the Mirror

day twenty-one

I Will Stay Free!

"It is for freedom that Christ has set us free. Stand firm, then, and do not let yourselves be burdened again by a yoke of slavery."

Galatians 5:1 (NIV)

Today is the final day! We have broken chains, closed doors, recovered, and been affirmed. Now, we can finally say that we are free! Here's the real challenge: STAYING FREE! Staying free is a daily process. It takes 21 days to break a habit, but afterward, we must maintain our freedom to ensure that the habit stays broken. Remember, the power of life and death is in our tongues. A major part of staying free is watching what we say. If you catch yourself speaking or thinking negatively, fight back with the Word of God.

After God sets us free, our only responsibility is to walk in our freedom. We do this by no longer being tempted to respond, act, partake in, or indulge in the things that once held us captive. We can get assistance with our walk of freedom from Christian counselors, our spiritual leaders, and others we know who believe and live by the Word of God. We don't have to walk alone. However, don't get lazy and depend on others for everything. It's always great to ask for prayer, but YOU can pray for yourself! YOU can speak life into yourself. On this journey called life, we must encourage ourselves sometimes. We won't always have a coach or a support team on the sidelines cheering us on. We must learn how to encourage ourselves from within. Well, that's it. I'm so proud of you for sticking with this devotional! Freedom looks great on you!

PRAYER STARTER Lord, thank You for setting me free! Now that I'm free, I want to stay free. Teach me how to stay free, stay in my purpose, stay in forgiveness, choose peace, and continuously love myself and others. Help me and teach me to kill my flesh daily. Increase my discernment. Help me realize what's good for me and what isn't. I understand that my freedom isn't just for me. It is also for my family, friends, and the generation that will follow me. God, I give You praise! I can finally look at myself in the mirror and see the person beyond the mirror. Thank You for allowing me to see the beautiful person you have created.

BTM CHALLENGE On this walk with God, accountability is a must! Find an accountability partner. Help each other to stay accountable for staying free. Be sure that your accountability partner is someone you trust and are comfortable with. Don't forget to journal your walk daily!

Journaling Beyond the Mirror

Scriptures for Affirmation

Beyond the Mirror isn't quite over yet! Below are a few scriptures you can use for daily affirmation. Challenge yourself to meditate on one scripture daily. Remember, I love you, you love you, but God loves you most! Be confident, be bold. May you always smile when you look beyond the mirror.

Psalm 46:1
Mark 6:21
Isaiah 43:7
Psalm 9:9
Micah 6:8
1 Corinthians 2:7
Galatians 4:6
Isaiah 55:11
1 John 3:1
Proverbs 3:1
Romans 6:4
2 Peter 1:3
Philippians 2:5
Genesis 1:27

Stay Connected

Thank you for purchasing Beyond the Mirror! Michal wants to stay connected with you! Below are a few ways you can reach out to Michal Renee. For more information about Michal Renee and Beauty for Ashes, visit www.iammichalrenee.wix.com/beyondthemirror.

INSTAGRAM @iammichalrenee

FACEBOOK Michal Renee

PERISCOPE @michalrenee_mua

EMAIL mlogan1211@gmail.com

50767083R00065

Made in the USA
Columbia, SC
16 February 2019